Jazz is American. It reaches every corner of the world. Performers interpret it differently. Yet it retains its unmistakable rhythmic, harmonic and melodic profile. It pictures the warmth of New Orleans. And, it relates the 'cool sound' with the tempo of the big city. THE JOY OF JAZZ depicts jazz development through the works of great personalities. For the first time simplified arrangements of Charlie Parker, Kid Ory, Thelonious Monk and Fats Waller are available to the student For the piano teacher and student this is not a frivolous excursion into the 'pop' field. It can be integrated with the regular teaching repertoire with excellent results. A few hints: Keep a steady beat throughout. Use little or no pedal. Play in the style.

Distributed throughout the world by Hal Leonard
Hal Leonard
7777 West Bluemound Road, Milwaukee, WI 53213
Email: info@halleonard.com

Hal Leonard Europe Limited
42 Wigmore Street, Marylebone, London WIU 2RY
Email: info@halleonardeurope.com

Hal Leonard Australia Pty. Ltd.
4 Lentara Court, Cheltenham, Victoria 9132, Australia
Email: info@halleonard.com.au

Love Somebody

Gerald Martin

Get Out Of Here

Kid Ory
Bud Scott

Lively "Dixieland" tempo

Won't Ya Come Out Tonight

Gerald Martin

Willy The Weeper

Denes Agay

Lady Bird

Arr. by
Frank Owens

Tad Dameron

Ev'ry Night
(Folk Blues)

Denes Agay

The Happy Organ

Ken Wood
David Clowney
James Kriegsmann

Maple Leaf Rag

Scott Joplin

Yes Indeed

Arr. by
Frank Owens

Sy Oliver

With a spirited beat

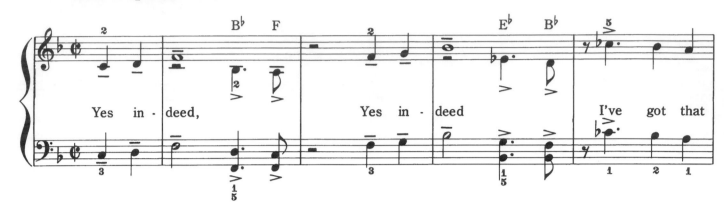

Yes in - deed,　Yes in - deed　I've got that

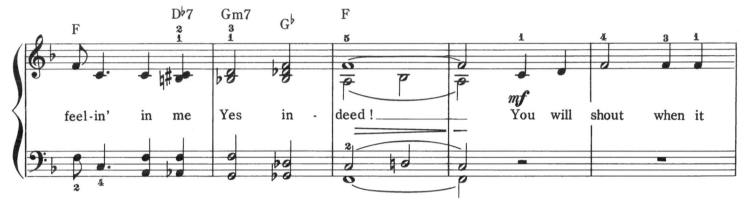

feel-in' in me　Yes in - deed !　You will shout when it

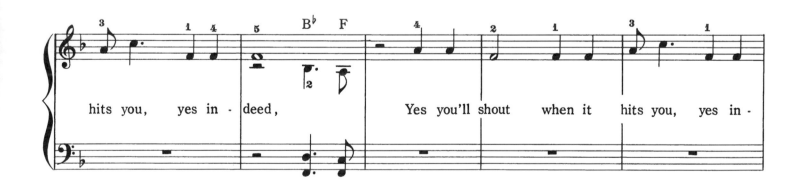

hits you,　yes in - deed,　Yes you'll shout　when it　hits you,　yes in -

deed,　When the spir - it　moves you,　You'll shout "Hal - le -

lu - jah,"   When it hits you   you   hol-la "Yes in - deed!"

Stomping Down Broadway

Ernest Wilkins

Medium jump tempo

Blue Petals

Robert Dorough

Slowly, but rhythmically

Kicking The Blues

Ernest Wilkins

24

Opus One

Sy Oliver

Moderate jump tempo

Lop-Pow

"Babs" Brown

Well Groomed

Charlie Shavers

J. D.'s Boogie Woogie

Jimmy Dorsey
Marvin Wright

Moderate boogie tempo

Easy Does it

Dave Martin

Sneakin' Home

Thomas "Fats" Waller

Things To Come

Dizzy Gillespie

Oop Bop Sh-bam

Dizzy Gillespie

Lively jump

52nd Street Theme

Fast

Thelonious Monk

Three Jazz Flavors

Moderate swing
"Salt Butter"

Erskine Butterfield

Slower with a lilt
"Sweet Butter"

Crisp and lively
"Peanut Butter"

Anthropology

Dizzy Gillespie
Charlie Parker

Palm Garden

Thomas "Fats" Waller

Slow blues tempo

Rollin' Rocks

Robert Dorough